HOUSTON TEXANS

ALL-TIME GREATS

BY TED COLEMAN

Book design by Jake Slavik
Cover design by Jake Slavik

Photographs ©: Mark J. Terrill/AP Images, cover (top), 1 (top); Jason Fochtman/The Courier/AP Images, cover (bottom), 1 (bottom); Bob Levey/NFL Photo Library/Getty Images Sport/Getty Images, 4; Scott Halleran/Getty Images Sport/Getty Images, 6; Bill Baptist/Getty Images Sport/Getty Images, 8; Bob Levey/Getty Images Sport/Getty Images, 10; Wesley Hitt/Getty Images Sport/Getty Images, 12; Steven Ryan/Getty Images Sport/Getty Images, 14; Rob Leiter/Getty Images Sport/Getty Images, 15; Scott Cunningham/Getty Images Sport Classic/Getty Images, 16; Thomas B. Shea/Getty Images Sport/Getty Images, 18; Frederick Breedon/Getty Images Sport/Getty Images, 20

Press Box Books, an imprint of Press Room Editions.

ISBN
978-1-63494-426-7 (library bound)
978-1-63494-443-4 (paperback)
978-1-63494-476-2 (epub)
978-1-63494-460-1 (hosted ebook)

Library of Congress Control Number: 2021916602

Distributed by North Star Editions, Inc.
2297 Waters Drive
Mendota Heights, MN 55120
www.northstareditions.com

Printed in the United States of America
012022

ABOUT THE AUTHOR

Ted Coleman is a sportswriter who lives in Louisville, Kentucky, with his trusty Affenpinscher, Chloe.

TABLE OF CONTENTS

CARR
8
TEXANS
8

CHAPTER 1
QUARTERBACKS AND BLOCKERS

The Houston Texans were a brand-new team in 2002. That year, they selected **David Carr** with the first pick in the draft. Carr served as the team's quarterback for five years. He showed improvement over his first few seasons. Unfortunately for Texans fans, the team couldn't find a way to surround him with talent.

One problem was the number of sacks Carr took. In three of his first four seasons, he was sacked more than any quarterback in the National Football League (NFL). It took a while for the Texans to find some star linemen.

Veteran center **Chris Myers** brought stability to the line in 2008. At one point, he started 112 games in a row for the Texans. He also earned two trips to the Pro Bowl.

Left tackle **Duane Brown** arrived the same year as Myers. However, Brown was a rookie in 2008. It took him a few years to improve his blocking skills. But over time, he grew into one of the league's best linemen.

Quarterback **Matt Schaub** came to Houston in 2007. He ended up setting all of the team's major passing records. Schaub was just a third-round pick when the Atlanta Falcons drafted him in 2004. But as a Texan, he got a chance to start. In 2009, Schaub led the team to its first winning season. And in 2011, he helped Houston reach the playoffs.

THE MIRACLE OF T.J. YATES

T.J. Yates began the 2011 season as Houston's third-string quarterback. However, injuries to the other two quarterbacks forced Yates into action late in the year. Yates started the first playoff game in team history. He even led Houston to a victory over the Cincinnati Bengals.

RYANS
59
TEXANS
59

CHAPTER 2

TEXAS-SIZED DEFENSE

On the defensive side of the ball, the Texans got a big boost in 2006. Linebacker **DeMeco Ryans** burst onto the scene as Defensive Rookie of the Year. Ryans settled into a role as a reliable tackler in the middle of the field. He made two Pro Bowls during his six seasons with Houston.

The Texans had another well-known rookie in 2006. Defensive end **Mario Williams** was chosen first overall in that year's draft. Williams proved to be a great pass rusher. He didn't miss a game until 2010. Just like Ryans, he made two Pro Bowls as a Texan.

JACKSON
25
TEXANS
25

The linebacker position soon became a strength for the Texans. In 2009, **Brian Cushing** won Defensive Rookie of the Year. That was just the start of a great career. Cushing recorded three 100-tackle seasons in his nine years with the Texans. Cushing also became known as a team leader.

In the early 2010s, Houston's defense became one of the best in the NFL. Cornerback **Kareem Jackson** was known as a punishing hitter. He was also great in coverage. During his nine years with the Texans, Jackson pulled down 16 interceptions.

BOB MCNAIR

The Texans are not the first NFL team to call Houston home. The Oilers played there from 1960 to 1996. However, they moved to Tennessee and became the Titans. Businessman **Bob McNair** wanted to bring another NFL team to Houston. His plan worked, and the league gave Houston a new franchise. McNair owned the Texans until his death in 2018.

WATT
99

In 2011, cornerback **Johnathan Joseph** joined Jackson in the secondary. Joseph made the Pro Bowl in his first two seasons with Houston. He also grabbed 17 interceptions. That was the most in team history.

Defensive end **J.J. Watt** was the final piece of the puzzle. Watt went on to set most of the team's defensive records. He also became one of the NFL's top pass rushers. In 10 seasons with Houston, Watt won three Defensive Player of the Year awards. He led the league in sacks twice. Watt was also a beloved figure in the Houston community for his charity work.

STAT SPOTLIGHT

CAREER SACKS

TEXANS TEAM RECORD

J.J. Watt: 101

Linebacker **Whitney Mercilus** made the defense even stronger when he arrived in 2012. Mercilus showed no mercy in chasing down quarterbacks. Mercilus recorded a career-high 12 sacks in 2015. He and Watt combined for 29.5 of the team's 45 sacks that season.

Jadeveon Clowney was next in a long line of standout Texans pass rushers. Clowney was the first overall pick in 2014. He showed steady improvement over his five seasons in Houston. He didn't end up as a sack master like Watt. But he still managed to hit quarterbacks and tackle runners for a loss of yardage.

JOHNSON
80
Riddell
80

CHAPTER 3
OFFENSIVE WEAPONS

Wide receiver **Andre Johnson** played with both David Carr and Matt Schaub. No matter who was throwing the ball, Johnson was the team's top playmaking threat. He didn't quite reach 1,000 receiving yards in his rookie year of 2004. But he hit that mark seven times in the next ten seasons.

STAT SPOTLIGHT

CAREER RECEIVING YARDS

TEXANS TEAM RECORD

Andre Johnson: 13,597

FOSTER
23

Another reliable target during this era was tight end **Owen Daniels**. Daniels was just a fourth-round pick in 2006. But he became one of the best tight ends in Texans history. Daniels regularly ranked among the team leaders in catches. He wasn't a deep threat like Johnson. However, Daniels could get open and provide a good option to the quarterback. He racked up 4,617 receiving yards in his eight years with the Texans. Only Johnson had more.

The receivers didn't do it all, though. In the 2010s, running back **Arian Foster** led Houston's ground game. Foster wasn't even drafted out of college. The league's other 31 teams soon regretted not signing him. After a slow start in 2009, Foster exploded for 1,616 yards in 2010. That season, he led the NFL in rushing yards and touchdowns.

Foster was a smooth runner. His quick cuts left defenders grabbing air. Foster went on to have three more 1,000-yard seasons during his seven years with the Texans. He led the NFL in touchdowns again in 2012.

The Texans picked up receiver **DeAndre Hopkins** in the 2013 draft. Hopkins learned some valuable lessons from Andre Johnson, who was near the end of his career. The speedy Hopkins proved to be just as dangerous as Johnson was. Hopkins spent seven years with the Texans. During that time, he recorded five 1,000-yard seasons. Hopkins was traded in 2020. So, he didn't get the chance to break Johnson's team records. Houston fans hoped their next star receiver was just around the corner.

LEADING SCORER

Kicker **Kris Brown** was the first kicker in Texans history. He stayed with the team through the 2009 season. During that time, Brown made 172 field goals and 251 extra points. That made him the team's all-time leading scorer. He racked up a total of 767 points for the Texans.

TIMELINE

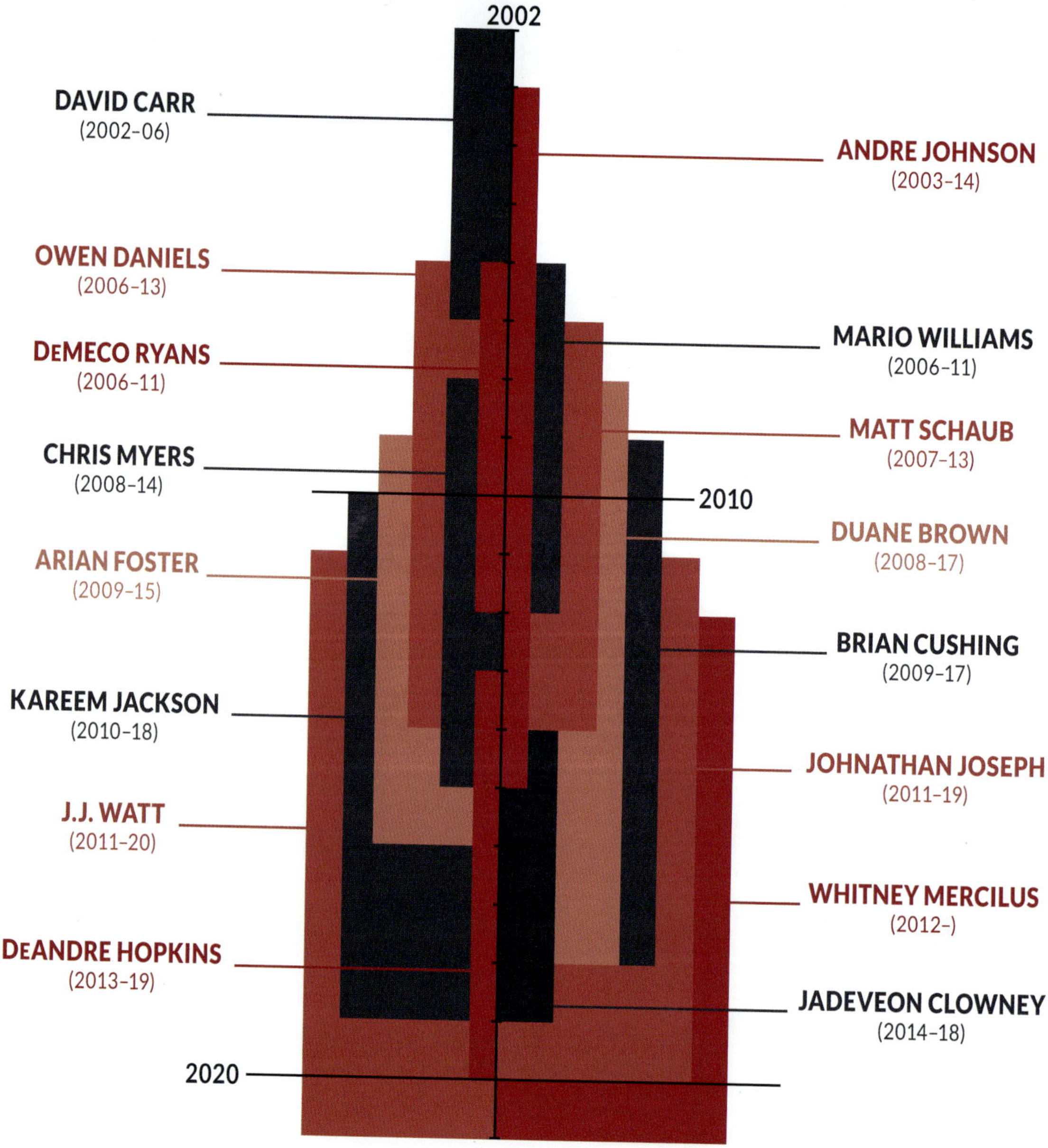
2002
DAVID CARR
(2002–06)
ANDRE JOHNSON
(2003–14)
OWEN DANIELS
(2006–13)
DeMECO RYANS
(2006–11)
MARIO WILLIAMS
(2006–11)
MATT SCHAUB
(2007–13)
CHRIS MYERS
(2008–14)
2010
DUANE BROWN
(2008–17)
ARIAN FOSTER
(2009–15)
BRIAN CUSHING
(2009–17)
KAREEM JACKSON
(2010–18)
JOHNATHAN JOSEPH
(2011–19)
J.J. WATT
(2011–20)
WHITNEY MERCILUS
(2012–)
DeANDRE HOPKINS
(2013–19)
JADEVEON CLOWNEY
(2014–18)
2020

TEAM FACTS

HOUSTON TEXANS

Founded: 2002

Super Bowl titles: 0*

Key coaches:

Gary Kubiak (2006–13), 61–64–0

Bill O'Brien (2014–20), 52–48–0

MORE INFORMATION

To learn more about the Houston Texans, go to **pressboxbooks.com/AllAccess**.

These links are routinely monitored and updated to provide the most current information available.

**1966 through 2020*

GLOSSARY

cornerback
A defensive player who covers wide receivers near the sidelines.

franchise
A sports organization.

linebacker
A player who lines up behind the defensive linemen and in front of the defensive backs.

rookie
A professional athlete in his or her first year of competition.

sack
A tackle of the quarterback behind the line of scrimmage.

secondary
The defensive players who typically cover wide receivers.

INDEX